D1373225

Buried in the Suburbs

poems

Jamie Lynn Heller

2018
Woodley Press
Washburn University
Topeka, Kansas

ISBN 978-0-9987003-2-8

Woodley Press
Washburn University
Topeka, Kansas

Dedicated to Lawrence and Johanna Miller,
their farm, and all of the lessons and wonderments
it encompassed.

Acknowledgements

I would like to thank the editors and publishers of the following books, journals, magazines, websites, and contests for their support.

150 Kansas Poems Website – "Castle Rock, Kansas"
805 Lit+Art – "Seashell" (Best of the Net nominee 2016)
Because I Said So: Poems on the Happiness and Crappiness of Parenthood – "Fired"
Blueline – "Spring Breezes", "When the leaves thin"
Burningword Literary Journal – "On a Chilled Wind", "thawing", "there is a place", "What Once Was"
The Frontier: Poetry Collection – "In Suburbia", "Make Way", "On the Prairie"
Flint Hills Review – "A Mouthful", "Fluttering"
I-70 Review – "Breath", "Butterflies", "New to the Nursing Home"
Iodine Poetry Journal – "The Inevitability of Touch"
Kansas City Voices – "An Entire Life"
KC Parent Magazine – "Not Alone"
Kansas Voices Contest Honorable Mention 2011 – "The minute hand fell off my clock"
Kansas Poets Website – "Kansas August Evening", "Kansas Rides"
Kudzu House Quarterly – "Waiting for Rain"
Little Balkans Review – "Ancestors", "Window Seat" (Pushcart Prize Nominee 2014)
Main Street Rag - "Clarity", "Kansas City, 1980s"
The Mom Egg Review – "I Denied Her"
Mothers Always Write – "Canoeing", "I'm talking to Grandpa, she tells me"
Noctua Review – "Margins"
Paddock Review – "An Entire Life"
The Storyteller Magazine – "Choices"

Tallgrass Voices: Poems – "Kansas Rides", "Vision from the
        Backseat Window"
Tule Review – "Within"
Whistling Shade – "Civilized"
Wilderness House Literary Review – "A Stranger's Hands, Her
        Hands", "Box of Rocks", "Button Jar", "Castle Rock,
        Kansas", "Flour Sack Dresses", "Hijacked Memories",
        "My Father's Sister", "My good intention"
Words Dance – "Behind Closed Doors"
Written River – "Adrift", "Anchor Me"

Table of Contents

Part III   /   57

Foreword

I'm glad to have read these poems. I'm also proud to write a bit about them here. Jamie Lynn Heller is an exuberant, clear-eyed writer who could teach us all a few literary tricks, and her poetry, as displayed previously in her excellent *Domesticated* (Finishing Line Press, 2015), is very much an extension of the poet herself: pithy, often wry, and intensely invested in conscience without compromise. The book you hold in your hands, her newest collection, possesses each of these qualities in spades.

Buried in the Suburbs easily turns over rocks that many might argue are too cumbersome to hoist. Right smack out of the gate Jamie is unwilling to blithely coexist with "our little / automatic robots / that allow us to / remain oblivious." This is a useful stubbornness, as we shamble about in a world where the things we've made have outsourced our good fortune: luck is of no consequence when we can open an app to pinpoint the arrival of rain or, quite literally, the road less traveled by. Timely and measured, *Buried in the Suburbs* reaffirms that like Jamie, we can go out to find our own luck—or even create a little ourselves.

It doesn't take long to notice that a key piece of Jamie's work is her steady awareness of nature. She knows full well that if we'd stop trying to subvert it, we could learn a few things from its older, wilder wisdom. Like fellow Kansas poets Steven Hind, Denise Low, and William Stafford, Jamie is not only a "nature poet"; when this collection's pieces discuss the world, our place within it is not as observers only, but as ornery students who have a heck of a lot to learn. Nature grows our very language, lest we forget: "when we need reminding, / the wild vine will wind its way" into our alliterative, indebted lives.

But let's face it: sometimes forgetting our place in the world is all too easy. Most of us know this hard fact very well. We get out over our skis, hitting the rocks we should've flipped from our path long ago. Jamie calls out the modern human process at large for every tree made a "questioning Y" by landscaping and urges patience as the clearest path to deciphering the whisper of bluestem and the "delicate power" of butterflies.

Importantly, in these poems Jamie doesn't shy away from leveling tough truths about intimacy in its many forms. She knows that if relationships are indeed houses we build, the windows "need washing / inside and out." To encourage good fortune, connections for Jamie must be resonant and mutual: not the "ghost of touch," but the kind that permits sardonic responses to lost articles of clothing, the kind that "steam the mirror."

Maybe most striking is the familiarity she finds wherever she happens to be. Despite the muscle memory of daily demands and activities, she imagines stopping along the road and walking through "a stranger's fields." No strangers are really strangers here, she seems to suggest. The fields belong first to themselves, and only afterward to all of us, when we are worthy.

I hope that you savor these poems, and meander through them with abandon. I hope you lean in to hear them as they plink into place like a careful line of water drops. In *Buried in the Suburbs*, Jamie Lynn Heller shows us hidden natural rhythms, like the keen droplets of rain that we sometimes miss.

—**Tyler Robert Sheldon**, author of *Traumas*
January 2018, Baton Rouge

Part I

Quietly We Become

"... trapped in the amber of the moment."
                                        -Kurt Vonnegut

Walking in borrowed minutes,
with keys to rented rooms
adding jingled notes
to steps we've already taken,
we rediscover a world
that's been wrung dry
and declare that
it is our very own.

Quietly we become
petrified, unable to recall
the details, holding on
to only what we happen
to have with us.

We are what
fills in spaces.

Seashell

When the day surges,
tugs at my ankles,
laps at my thighs,

I escape to fields
of cracked clay,
sun bleached bones,

and hide from the shelter
of a passing cloud.

Even in this place I carry
the sound of the ocean
with each breath.

The roar of its waves
caught in a seashell
lodged in my throat.

In Suburbia

where we are not capable
of checking the weather app
and realizing we could
turn off
our automatic sprinkles when it rains
so they pour
both of them
the sky and our little
automated robots
allowing us to
remain oblivious

Civilized

When we need reminding,
the wild vine will wind its way
under the back deck,
through the gap
by the doormat and bloom.
Drips of rain will squeeze
through cement and pool
together in the basement.
Sparrows will move
into the dryer vent.
Ants will greet us
on the kitchen counter.

Make Way

Maples striping the avenue
have been trained to grow
between sidewalk and street
and around an aerial electrical highway.

They have been snipped and trimmed
shaping a line of questioning Ys
swaying timidly in the breeze
and in the tight space
we've granted them.

Caught

The tuft of white fur
at the tip of each ear
on the black ally cat,

the yellow feathers
under the throat
of a scolding bird

find me, insist
on an introduction.

I put their burden on
one shoulder at a time.

The splash of purple on
solid red petals of weeds
growing from asphalt,

the tender white of a bud
on a cracking branch
of browned petals

follow me through
days I long to be hazy.

I envy those who simply
walk through it all.

Because the crispness
of table edges, the
depth of ink on pages,

the brush stroke of
brown escaping from
my left iris, keep me,
hold me still.

Butterflies

Between chilly spots of shade,
in one of the bright patches
of morning sunshine
where the dew had already let go,
a blanket of butterflies
made the dirt road shimmer.
Shades of brown and white
swirled along their wings
as they slowly opened and closed,
each with its own rhythm.
Our approaching truck forced them
reluctantly, sleepily, a foot or so
in the air, far enough for us to see
tire tracks made of their dead
where others had already driven.
They were a skirt, caught by the wind,
briefly exposing fresh scars on young legs.
We didn't debate about what to do.
He just shifted gears, turned the wheels,
took us off the road, onto the grass,
around their delicate power.

Walking on Sand Dunes in the Rain

On sandy undulations,
each drip its own sound,
cooling rain winds itself
around minute grains,
enclosing dryness.

Our steps break
the new resistance of a crust,
bury our feet
in warmth trapped
from the morning's sun.

The small mounds of sand
our steps displace
hold their peaks
until the rain soothes
their edges, rolling down
stones one by one

to rest upon
the blanket of themselves,
healing the disturbance,

and we have no longer
been there.

and yet

there is space
for another lick,
for another twist of the cap
on the etched swirls of
the bottle's lip,
for the thin tendril's growth
on the pocked surface
of a boulder,
for another on the bench
at the February bus stop,
December church pew
if we all nudge to the left,
for the glimmer of question
in the heart
of contented loneliness
while watching an eagle land
in a greening field
and cock its head
to look us in the eye

What Whispers in the Night

In the darkness,
sounds skip easily
across the porcelain
of cooler air.
In this hushed place
small things
have their say,
house creaks, mouse
shuffles, fears
and dreams
get their due.

Anchor Me

Anchor me to the shore
where the tides bring satin sands
to smother soothingly
and waves tease my toes
with cool promises of depths.

Anchor me in the woods
to my grandfather's saplings
grown and sheltering now,
intricately woven branches
draw shade for tenderness to grow.

Anchor me loosely in the open fields
where the winds come to play,
coaxing my unreeling spirit
to drift in their courses,
my hair flowing like rivers.

Anchor me in prairie grasses,
tender blades waving long
in a dry wind,
roots reaching deeply
in welcoming earth.

Anchor me securely
in the warmth of you
where night's blanket curves
over my chilled shoulders,
slips under my chin.

What We May Miss

The smaller leaves,
edges striving
for symmetry,
their startling shades
turned over to lie
against the sidewalk,
our sheltered girls
feigning shyness,
flutter teasingly
the colors of themselves
in a passing breeze.

Living in Dryness

I search for handles
in the day, catches
of sunlight, first buds
that propose the affections
of the world, use a stranger's
smile as a hand hold
on the desert mesa of routine,
look for what I need to see
beyond the reality of cacti
and choked air.

Chasing Rain

And I know I cannot,
with the scent of moisture
heavy on this day,
just continue my route.

Instead, I walk the long way,
across ridge lines
and dip into dry gullies
until I feel the intensity
of sunlight drape
on bared shoulders
and the first stirrings
of a breeze curve
along my neck.

I walk until
shafts of grey bind
themselves to the ground,
until rain blown to me
by sharp winds
dilutes the layers
of dust on my skin.

Red Tail at Sunset

Gripping winter branches,
as bared and crooked
as his own talons,
he is caught in the horizon.
Unruffled by other's presence
with wind gliding along his feathers,
his stare fixes
on what is his alone.
Using highways and their travelers
as his personal flushers,
he waits for small movements
that betray hidden hosts
and signal he can glide
into the dried roadside grasses
to claim a meal.

Vision from the Backseat Window

on a crouching hillside
covered with defrocked oaks
a lone birch
reaches bare white limbs towards the sky
an embodied spirit
rooted in the graveyard of winter
daring passing passengers to give it a try

there is a place

there is a place between
awake and conscious
that is not easily torn

a place encircling
intent and movement
that clings to stillness

a place connecting
forgiving and forgetting
that slips thoughts

where we get caught
in the light of dead stars

Acknowledgement

Frost finds the fallen corn stalks,
every waver on tree bark,
barbs and their long stretches of wire,
grass blades allowed to grow long
or clipped close,
the newest twig,
missed by sun,
tucked in
among its brethren.

thawing

the first sighing movements
heralding a warm breeze
as winter's first tear lets go,
the yielding of the night's
warbling notes to new tones,
the brushing of a reach
in the womb,
a sparrow catching
an updraft,
a waver bringing
a chance I can,
for a grasp,
feel the earth rolling

Spring Breezes

The first warmth presses
against my clothes with the tentative
touch of adolescent hands
before running off
to perch, giggling, in new branches,
wrapping itself around purple buds.

Part II

Kansas August Evening

Open my window, Mommy
she said
I want to hear the
cicada lullaby

Kansas Rides

I gripped the under curve of metal
lining the bed of his farm-battered truck
to keep from getting
tossed out
and lost in the prairie sea.
The hot wind in my hair
carried the breath of the land in bloom and
hours later in bed my pillow would
absorb the scent
to keep me company.
I could see the bald curve of his head
through the back window,
the tip of a toothpick pricked his silhouette,
one hand on the wheel,
his left arm, from shirt sleeve to watchband,
a long-time partner of the sun's.
It didn't matter where he went
or what chore waited,
I went along and
rode the fields.

Margins

You freely interrupted,
not at all concerned with
stomping all over budding love,
my latest fling. Your un-asked for
analysis and disbelief in fate,
squeezed between lines, dripped
into the margins, bled black ink
onto my conversation with
Mr. Darcy, hijacking my reading time
as effectively as a hypnotist
attaching a pocket watch chain
to my attention. Instead of following
the neat trail of printed text, I'm off the path,
tracking you, wondering when you
found this story, where you traveled with it,
why you used a pen in this spot
and a pencil in others, how you might
have held the book with one hand splaying
the spine open, or gently with both,
and what your palms felt like against
the cover, because your breath lingers on
the pages from when you leaned forward and
wrote in my margins.

Kansas City, 1980's

To the background music
of atoms splitting, I rolled
my uniform skirt each morning.
Talk of Reagan and Russia chilled
adults with a very different thrill
than rippled through me
when my latest fantasy and I
locked gazes over our social studies books.

The same mouths that discussed
the prospects of World War III asked
what I wanted to be when I grew up,
and while trying to blink away the images
from *The Day After*, I intentionally left
the second button on my shirt undone,
later to hide my dipped neckline
in embarrassment after a boy tried
to look and our teacher threw
an eraser in frustration
because we weren't listening.

Castle Rock, Kansas

He climbed up through history once buried,
petrified layers of an ancient sea,
his undeterred energy conquered all
eighty feet with only his hands and untried will
as he grappled with a tower
standing against wind-owned plains

while our teacher, his veins bulging
through skin settling comfortably into age
and full of a stronger vintage, waited
with his field worn boot propped on a fallen boulder,
waited for what he knew this boy would find at the top,
what would, cackling in his ear, pop his bravado,
alert him to his place in the world,

and when it was time, the man
stepped forward, slapped billows of fine chalk powder
from his faded jeans, adjusted his hat, looked straight up
at the boy clutching the top
of a precarious table,
and then calmly, soothingly,
talked him down.

A Mouthful

When I open my mouth to respond
after just one bite
of his homemade divinity
mixed with glass shards, egg whites,
casual words and corn syrup,

my teeth begin to crumble,
spring free of their bed,
flounder on my tongue, fall
into my cupped hand.

He looks at me, politely
waiting a moment, but all
my words are being chewed,
chopped and snagged
on enameled boulders.

I fill both my pockets with incisors
and my purse with molars
while trying not to choke

as new ones sprout and fall again
until I wrap my lips
around them securely,
keep my jaw clamped tightly,
resorting to headshakes and

hair tossing nods
while he smiles

impressed with my
listening skills.

My Son Can't Find His Hat

It is sitting in the middle of the kitchen table.

I am on one side with my bowl of cereal.
He is standing on the other, obviously
in a hurry and unappreciative
of my response that,
"Yes, I've seen it."

But I've decided, for fun,
to see how many times
he'll ask me where it is.

He's up to four so far.

My good intention

gathered dust on the merchant copy of a receipt,
resting on the desk near the other bills,

the tip carefully-calculated a little high,
my signature a little hurried.

I remember she was surprisingly young
for us to have daughters the same age,
was cheerful and attentive
without being intrusive, and we
were rushing on to somewhere else.

The receipt that should have let her know
we appreciated her
landed in my wallet by mistake
as we gathered everything and moved on,

then was transferred to the desk where I thought
I'd see it and remember to drop it by
the next time we were out, because

the credit card statement showed only
the meal and taxes, nothing for her but
my good intention on a very thin slip of paper.

My Father's Sister

She'd rustled on the periphery
of my childhood, an aunt who once gave me
a red sucker after I skinned my knee.

Today she's a guest in my home, a guest in my life
I wish would stay long enough to take off her shoes
and learn where the silverware drawer is.

We hurry around the kitchen, in each other's way.
Trying to be familiar, but we haven't
learned a rhythm yet.

I place on her the burden
of carrying answers to my questions
about a man I didn't really know.

At his name she shakes her head,
halfway smiles and doesn't finish
the sentence, "Your father was..."

So he just was.

But when we stop for a moment in our circles,

her hand rests next to mine on the counter,
our skin tones match, finger bones angle

along similar tracks, and I don't need
her words anymore to know my hair will turn white
instead of grey as age spots sprout between our freckles.

Climbing a Tree in a Lightning Storm

Because the small plane was caught in the top branches
and he and his dad had put it together just the two of them
at the kitchen table covered in bright plastic pieces
and they'd laughed when the rubber band engine snapped
and then raced each other around the house to find a
replacement
and the little plane actually flew outside on that bright day
and mom called them her "pilots" while she snapped pictures
and when he ran off to the neighbor's to retrieve it
and they didn't think he was looking
dad slid his arm around her waist and kissed her neck
and she'd laughed with her whole body and if
he could just climb
a little higher
today if
the windblown
branches would
embrace and
boost him
he could
reach the plane
take it back
to them
and it would
fly again
breaking apart
the storm
that had moved
inside.

The Inevitability of Touch

We drip our lives behind us
with every step, every lingering touch
on a spring budded branch,
every breath trailing in the breeze
intermingling with it all

Not Alone

one pink flip-flop in the kitchen
silverware drawer still open
half-eaten purple Popsicle pooling on the counter
TV on
topless Playdough still moist
toilet not flushed (no paper on the roll)
school papers sliding down the steps
a stuffed animal maze in the hall
missing blue-handled scissors sticking out from under the linen
closet door
bathroom light on
three small papers detached from a bandage on the mat
damp towel clutching with one corner to the bar
dryer door open
clean clothes trailing along the tile
music from a bedside radio tinkling through the air
bedcovers caught in mid-sneak on their way to the floor
pajamas emptied and tossed across the desk
and although not another human can be found
I'm defiantly not alone.

Canoeing

She will remember a vast lake,
with deep water, ringed by a wild wood.
As we make our way back and forth across the pond,
her paddle barely dips below the waterline.
The handle drags along the edge of the boat.
Sometimes she misses the water completely
as she oscillates between chatter
and mid-sentence stopping awe
when something splashes nearby.
I work to navigate us away from the shallows
while thinking of the immensity ahead for her,
hoping I will continue to sit behind
and watch her gasp in wonder of the sky, the breeze,
and the small creatures that make the brush rustle.

Fired

Left work late to start with,
rush hour traffic,
headache,
home.
White plastic tooth-shaped box on the counter,
eighth baby tooth with its bloody eroded root inside.
Dinner, cooked instead of ordered, is an accomplishment.
Soccer practice, (oh so typical I know)
homework,
baths,
medicine,
potty (2:35 am wet bed prevention for the smallest one),
bed for all.

Dog barfing on the carpet beats the alarm clock by
five minutes.
Breakfast, clothes, lunch money, hair and teeth, backpacks,
but
the tooth fairy
didn't make it.

The Worst in Me

All the scraps I'd scrubbed off the plate,
the crusts of hard bread, edges of cheese
with speckles of white mold, shrimp shells,
rib bones and chewed bits of gristle
safely deposited in the trash,
with a cross word from you
get ripped out of the bag and strewn
along the curbside for the neighbors to see.
Just your tone is enough
to unearth the bendable carrots,
the melted edges of spinach leaves,
the untouched peas gone cold and defiant,
the root tips from chives, banana peels and corn husks
I thought I'd wisely composted
so they could turn into
something useful instead of merely serving
as witness to my vanquished appetite, but
I've learned after many meals with you
to store the cranky broccoli
in the bottom drawer
in case I need it.

I Denied Her

I denied her
ice cream cones for many years.
Memories of anticipated sweetness
landing on hot, ant-sprinkled sidewalks
kept me insisting hers
would be served in a bowl.

I denied her
the lesson of licking softly, consciously
planning how to tackle a bump and balance
the whole on its precarious perch,
how to anticipate melting, the satisfaction

of licking the back of a hand
to get a runaway drop,
earning the crunch of the cone,
using her tongue
to get the last bits buried deep.

Walking with My Daughter

I didn't know the elusive taste
of what I'd try to blend for her,
for us, was just

standing beside her
as geese glide down,
one by one,
to the surface of this small pond.

As if I am staging the scene,
she looks from them to me,
to them, to me.
I reach for her hand,

this.

Ancestors

looking at their frozen faces
captured when they thought they should
look like painted portraits of royalty
it's hard to believe they lived in a world of color
a world of fabric and texture
of rain and wind
of sex and lust
of movement
of joy

when I imagine them right before and
after the exploding flash
I see them adjusting their dress
shaping a mustache
placing themselves for the pose
surrounded by a world tinted only in
shades of sepia

Rosary Beads at Night

She held her days,
each curve of an hour
fingered carefully,
each link tying a life together
in a march that circled
back around to promises
already echoed,
pleas already faded,
hopes already reached.

Flour Sack Dresses

When confusing the faces of her family
Seeing in them blends of strangers
Who seem familiar
Mixed with sudden flashes
Of young lovers and lost family
She closes her eyes and sinks into
Clear memories of summer grass under bare feet
Water pulled from a deep well on her lips
And the whispered touch of homemade dresses
Pieced from flour sacks bought at the general store
Their many patterns eventually sewn into quilts
And laid across her lap
To warm her now even on hot days

An Entire Life

There's nothing like

going through Great Aunt Priscilla's house
after hospice has removed its equipment
and you've donated the wheelchair,
found the walker, flushed the pills,
debated what to do with an opened package
of adult diapers and her prosthetic breasts,
opened the blinds and windows to let in light and air,
found her old set of dentures,
her package of hearing aid batteries,
her crazy beaded chain attached to her reading glasses,

and

discovering a
lacy red nightgown,
stuffed in the back of a drawer,
in a style a couple of decades old,
a couple of sizes too small,

to remind you of
her life
before

Button Jar

Grandma had a button jar,
its tin lid starting to rust. Within
the brightly colored bangles
were waiting to serve a purpose.
Some still held scraps of thread
from their last attachment, pieces
of someone's discarded day.

The ones made of bone or shell clinked
differently than the plastic buttons
as they rolled into each other
while I lined them up by color or size or story
she would tell about the last shirt he wore,
a baby's gown, the dress made for a special day.

Grandma had a button jar of memories
and it kept me busy while she patched
a barbed wire snag or reinforced a seam.

New to the Nursing Home

When I asked if I could
bring her anything,
she told me she wanted

a peach
like she remembered

easily bruised,
juice that made wasps hover,
tenderly filled with promises of him

walking by her father's store,
each morning he would
tip his hat and wink

her blush like peaches.

Hijacked Memories

"Remember how your sister
once snuck into my room
    "No, mother."
    I laid ironed shirts on the back of a nearby chair.
and covered her face
with my lipstick?
    "It wasn't her."
    She likes me to use the pink hangers for her shirts,
    the blue for her pants.
Oh, how frightened I was!
That she'd somehow burned herself -
    "But mother-"
    She gets upset if I don't
    put her clothes back in the correct order.
on my curlers! She was such
a beautiful, funny girl.
    "But mother, remember-"
    When she once discovered a shirt in the wrong
    place, they had to call the nurses in.
I always knew she'd make something of herself.
She had that spirit you know?"
    "it was me."
    I hope she doesn't notice
    she's one shirt short today.

A Stranger's Hands, Her Hands

Her hands were grandma's hands, and it startled me
to see them again.

The grey veins swelled from
their stream beds under dried skin,

knuckles bulged and slowly twisted
her fingers into bared tree branches.

The service ended, and
she rose to retrieve her purse,

a bulking old leather piece that had slipped
farther than she could reach under the pew.

I offered to get it for her. She smiled
and patted my arm gently.

I wanted to cup her hands in my own, kiss them,
hold them against my cheek.

I tried to think of something
to say

that would keep her
near me.

I faltered out
a flat statement.

She replied warmly
and walked away

while I mourned
each step she took.

Box of Rocks

When he found it again, he returned
the box to her. She had forgotten
about her rocks, carefully collected
for their sparkle or smooth coolness
until the feel of the box in her hands
tapped on her memory. She'd wanted
much more from him, but he'd
hung on to her rocks because
they belonged to

his little girl who used to play
in the shade under the oak he planted,
hold his hand, bring him pictures, and
the sound of her laughter dancing
in the house still playfully dashes
around the corners of his life.

Within

He yelled for me to grab the chain, there by the door,
resting near the hook he used to move rectangular bales.
       I remember
He looped the cold metal around two stumps beneath her tail.
       how he wrapped
Her bellows filled the morning, her neck pulsed
       that chain
as her eyes rolled away their color while he pulled.
       around me
A calf landed at his feet. And while
       and waited
many more calving seasons
       for me to pull.
weathered his hands, deep inside of him
new cells began a foundation.

One Last Drive

He waited until the house was full,
a fourth generation dodging around knees,
kitchen counters laden with warmth,
chatter pushing out the knowledge
that this would be the last of these
gatherings with everyone present.
The next year would be different.
As each person arrived and was hugged,
he told them he needed to check on the cattle,
they were in the back pasture, not far,
could he borrow their keys?
"Not now" or "I'm sure the cows are fine"
were the replies along with quick kisses
on his parched cheeks. They all knew
the herd was gone and had been for months.
When it was time to pray, the circle
of their clasped hands bulged out
of the kitchen, overflowed the dining room,
and looped through part of the living area.
When they waited too long for him
to start the blessing, they realized he was gone.
Out the front window Aunt May's burgundy Buick
bounced through the field. They thought
they'd hidden all the keys,
but he'd found one set and drove
as if he still owned the land.

I'm talking to Grandpa, she tells me

after taking a couple steps from the car,
the roadside weeds reaching for her,
she turns towards the open field.
Come on, I say, but
a recently harvested field
stretches to the horizon, dried
cornstalks rustle in the cooling air and

I look up into the blue of my father's eyes.
We've just laid him to rest outside the family town,
next to relatives, surrounded by the fields
he loved. The sound of my mother
telling him she wanted to lie next to him

replays in my ears as I watch
my child looking past a field,
her lips moving, but her voice snatched
out of reach by persistent wind.

Catching What He Ran Away From

He still smokes on the porch,
sleeps in the guest room
of the house that is now his,
puts the pans away where she always did,
steps into his father's boots,
shifts through the workbench,
tests the feel of old tools in his hands,
stumbles through fields he didn't plant,
checks the length of roots,
looks for the sky to drop.

Slipping

I need that place to stay
as the photograph I carry
in the soft folds of memory.
The paint won't peel
in the summer sun,
curls of cream.
The cat's litter won't
wander into the woods
stalking fat grasshoppers.
Wild vines will not reach
the garden gate and wind themselves
into a living latch.
The sapling will be
too young to bear fruit, always.
That one place
will stay the center
of my compass,
my tether in every field.

Part III

Living in the Tunnel

Routine creates a sheltered path.

The air in the house, the car, the

office, comfortably regulated.

The most efficient route to work

traversed with muscle memory.

Long days take me and bring me

home in a dark tunnel.

I can't confirm the sun rose.

I imagine

pulling over on

the side of

the road and

walking through

a stranger's fields.

When the leaves thin

I can see my neighbor
on down the way.

He looks up

and we hesitate, caught
between waving
or pretending the curtain

is still between us.

The minute hand fell off my clock

and the rest of its pieces
kept dutifully ticking away.
There was no reaching out of the hour hand,
no worried gaze from the numerals,
no slowing of the three fake gold plated orbs hanging below
as they spun left, then spun right, then left,
no alarm bouncing around inside the glass globe
that covers its little world
to alert all to the injury.
It was a wedding gift, out of place
in our décor, and we unquestioningly
replace its battery
like we water the plants,
dust the marriage,
but today the minute hand fell off my clock,
it lay like an exhausted recruit,
and nothing stopped to mind.

Fluttering

(to the too long caged)

It's their panic I feel,
these little birds too long in their cages,
on sale in stores, tucked and forgotten
in children's bedrooms, added to the corners
of carefully designed houses, their squeaks
and colors used like pillows or vases.

With their tiny hearts wound tightly,
an unexpected rustle of a breath
sets off a furious battle within the wire walls.
They fling feathers like stones,
that can't drop or sting, so float.

Despite my coaxing, they don't
settle on their perch or sing or fly away,
even after I've left the door open.

Maybe it scares them,
an open door,
the prospect of cats,
of children's gripping hands,
of staining the new divan,
of space.

Breath

Mourning the time I deny myself,
I steal minutes from drained routine
to watch rain-bent grasses
stretch themselves in the sun
where breezes can again
stroke their long blades, and
I remember to recognize
my breath as it enters, swirling
against my bloodstream,
and as it rushes away
losing itself in the morning.

Strung

On a wet, fall day,
air filled with mist
so thick it's neither
falling or rising,
a line of water drops
string themselves
along the under curve
of a too smooth branch.
Each partial drip
a twin of its neighbor,
each the same sized step apart,
each holding a miniature, inverted
reflection of the world,
the gentle order
behind the ease
of the everyday.

On a Chilled Wind

Winter comes to tell me to be still,
to stand and look out windows
onto landscapes scrubbed barren
by winds that round up the excess,
scraps of the discarded, imperfections,
are gently smoothed into graceful curves
by snow laid down piece by piece
on even the smallest twig.
Chills that tingle toes, crisp ears,
push me back into places
where blankets and warm drinks
invite me to sit down.

Waiting for Rain

Long corn leaves, dried
to brown, brittle ribbons

blow from a dead field
into the parking lot where

they scratch against blacktop,
catch under car tires.

Each dry breeze steels
moisture from farmer's hopes,

carries only laughter
from nearby kids kicking up

clouds of powdered earth
with their recess games.

Window Seat

alone in my room,
sent there or retreated to,
I'd stare out my open window,
lean my head against the frame
feel it press against me
and watch the clouds
bloom, roll, boil,
between the oaks towering
over the neighbors' houses and
the highway of power lines,
the sun would cling to the ground
its light altering with the strain
before it lost its grip.
I'd close my eyes
when the breeze snuck in and
felt its way around my face,
then wait for sounds of the storm's mood,
angry hard, proving a point
claiming the earth
the territory,
a satin sigh releasing everything,
or a collection of gentle excuses
passing through,
so now when the rain comes
my bones feel its build and
with the memory smell of metallic screen
enmeshed in my history,
I turn my face to the wind.

Choices

standing on tip toes
leaning just not too far out from the perch
with one hand anchored
the other shielding my eyes from the sun
I look over and wonder what I'd be doing
if I had climbed there
up one of the other branched
possibilities of my life

While My Hands Slowly Age

I watch the leaves grow
a little each day, starting
the morning I thought
it was too early for them
to be testing the air.
They jump forward, brushing
against my window in winds
that fight between the seasons.
Entranced by their change, I fail
to see dust gathering on the sill,
my hands needing lotion.

Adrift

Ice retreating
up the mountain
releases water
I confuse for sky.

Gripping the paddle
to keep from
slipping away, from
running across
surface tension while
avoiding consumption
in one swallow
from below
or above,

I strain, grasp
his voice through
the insistence of
lunch peaches, unheard
pleas, pine whispers,

and tether this place
within my reach.

Clarity

there's a clarity that comes
in the space between awake and not
a sudden simple flash of understanding
of purpose of plans
the just right lines and phrases
the next steps to take
the solution to some tangle
that suddenly stands free of bondage
before the mind slips further away
to play in lands of Dali's strokes

unless captured
on a nightstand notebook with a nearby pen
by morning the substance has dissolved
leaving granules of an answer
the lingering taste of possibility and
the belief in its existence
but no way to gather
the bouncing elements together
and create the vision again

Winter Rain

when it has been too long,
the first taps
startle, snag
conversations, wake the
drowsy, turn the ear

I had been waiting,
I had forgotten

when it has been too long
and the pounding
stops, the ceasing
allows me
a deep breath

I had been waiting,
I had forgotten

Not Today

There will be a day when I won't have to ask him if it's okay
to turn the air conditioning off, sleep with the window open. When
I'll just buy the new bedspread I want and paint the room blue
because my days will have returned to days of
I, no longer we

When there won't be a debate
about who can acquiesce more
while deciding a place to eat
because I'll only need to consult with
myself and not us

but please
not yet.

Setting up My Retirement Account

I asked for paint and canvas,
an easel and a room
with windows on all sides,
a view of water and mountains
at my finger tips
and brushes that tempt
art students to sneak in and slip
them into their oversized clothes.
My first work will be
from one thick tube of blue.
Using a brush with a single hair,
I'll apply a thousand strokes
of the sky's changing hues
while my tea grows cold
and streaks of sunlight
rotate around me.

Worry Stones

Each of my cares
with unique striations
clusters of colors
fits easily in my pocket
their gathered weight
adding small ounces
to my slowing stroll

Each fits comfortably
in my palm where my
fingers can choose one
or two as wanted
as needed and work
to smooth even
imagined variations

I can no longer discern where
the edge of me ends
and the stone begins

Standing on What Shouldn't Hold Me

With thoughts that tumble
and snag in bared branches,
I step out onto the ice.
When it doesn't crack,
I let go of the pier.

Winter hasn't been hard enough
to ruffle the water's surface.
Rust colored leaves curl to look
at the frozen halves of themselves
caught beneath the ice.

I watch one closely.
Its free half swaying
in the cold breeze while
its underwater half, stilled,
belongs to a different realm.

When my own
unwavering reflection
comes into focus,
I allow a tentative smile
before looking out
across the lake.

I never planned to
leave a pebble trail.
Just filled my pockets
with stones from the shoreline,
stood on water, and dared
for the thawing to begin.

What Once Was

An old photograph,
a startling scent,
a hesitant moment
of almost recognition

draws my finger tips
to the shallow pool
of that other time,

and it's colder
than I remember,

the liquid clutches,
pulls to stay with me
for a moment,
loses its grip and falls,
sending ripples
through the memory
of the me that once was
who knew the you
that no longer exists.

Behind Closed Doors

Now the table holds
only one plate
for its two chairs.
The window needs washing
from the inside and out.
The words are all clasped
shut in books or scattered
so far across the keyboard
tracing them would leave
a tangled web
to trap thoughts.
The ghost of your touch
isn't strong enough
to wrinkle the sheets,
steam the mirror,
unlock me.

On the Prairie

With the wind wrapped around me,
I let my hands fall
into the top fringes
of Bluestem from last summer,
dried now to a golden tone.
It whispers old stories
I cannot understand,
but can feel with a light
patient touch.

About the Author

Jamie Lynn Heller uses poetry as her caffeine. When words find each other at just the right moment, it is more energizing than soda, coffee, or strong tea. Jamie is a graduate of Kansas State University and the University of Missouri Kansas City. She is a Pushcart Prize nominee (*Little Balkans Review* 2014) and Best of the Net nominee (*805 Lit + Art* 2016). Her chapbook *Domesticated* was published in 2015 (Finishing Line Press). She received honorable mention awards in the *Whispering Prairie Press Writing Contest 2012,* and the *Kansas Voices Contest 2011, 2017.* For a complete list of publications see her webpage at jamielynnheller.blogspot.com.

About the Artist

Walt Cochran is a high school history teacher, varsity girls' soccer coach, dad, husband, church youth group mentor, and photographer. He enjoys his teaching job thoroughly but has a passion and gift for photography. When he is not at school, you can usually find him taking photos or fishing! He spends a lot of time in the outdoors and enjoys traveling and spending time with his family. See more of his work on his webpage at: https://www.waltcochranphotography.com/ .

Praise for *Buried in the Suburbs*

Jamie Lynn Heller has a wonderful ability to take her readers into the heart of each poem and invite us to participate fully with each experience. In so doing, we become part of the human story of our times, our places, whether canoeing across a lake, in its middle, experiencing "the sky, the breeze, and the small creatures that make the brush rustle," or riding in "the bed of a farm battered truck." She sets us in the middle of recognizable moments as if we are there. It is with pleasure that I invite you to experience Jamie's poems and the living truths they have to share.

—**Dan Pohl**, Author of *Autochthonous: Found in Place*

Jamie Lynn Heller's collection inspires me to look closer at the common items surrounding me, from book margins to flour sacks and many overlooked items. Heller's talent lies in how she shows us their beauty, their fragile nature or their usefulness and forces us to also remain just as present in the day-to-day tasks that we perform so unconsciously. Her pieces are witty, thought-provoking, entrancing and remind us that the mundane is where our lives are lived.

—**Gustave Adolfo Aybar**, author of *We Seek Asylum*

Jamie Lynn Heller's poems speak to the human experience from the rare position of understanding the reality of it all, with its inherent futility, and yet the poems are not jaded or resigned. *Buried in the Suburbs* is a book of life. The poems in this book speak to us all in myriad ways. The first poem in the book, "Quietly We Become," ends with the lines, "We are what/fills in the spaces," but these poems find exactly what is in all of life's hidden spaces in a way most writers only ever hope to expose.

—**James Benger**, author of *You've Heard It All Before*

Buried in the Suburbs is filled with images that come not only from suburbia, but also from the poet's wistful dialogues with nature, with memories, and with her innermost longings. She portrays these inner and outer worlds with depth, humor, and passion. The reader is immediately caught up in the poet's struggle to live an authentic life, to see things with clarity and truth. "We drip our lives behind us / with every step," she asserts, and we journey with her as she chronicles both the ordinary and extraordinary moments of life, recognizing, as Kim Addonizio says, that they are the same thing.

—**Maril Crabtree**, author of *Fireflies in the Gathering Dark*

Whether she is venturing out or staying close to home, Jamie Lynn Heller gives up poems made of insight and imagination. Like its author, this book lives in the suburbs but often steers us off the highway to walk through a stranger's fields or stand in a rainstorm. Heller writes about the power of love and memory with nostalgia, wry humor and sometimes a dash of horror. In Heller's suburbs—the staidest of environments— the wild is never far away. There are sparrows in the dryer vents and ants on the kitchen counters. This is also true in relationships shared with friends, lovers, and family members. *Buried in the Suburbs* is a tribute to where Heller is from—a place where the trappings of modern life don't always succeed in keeping prairie roots from breaking through the asphalt and tidy green laws.

—**Pat Daneman** author of *After All and Where the World Begins*